mexican bar

The editor wishes to thank Édouard Collet, Christine Martin and Mélanie Joly

for their valuable aid and Marine Barbier for her careful reading.

casual mexican cooking at home

mexican bar

Marie-Caroline Malbec

Photographs by Jean-Charles Vaillant
Design by Marie-Caroline Malbec

[When the flavors blend…]

To everyone's delight, national borders are slowly disappearing in matters of cuisine. As the new century gets underway, we're witnessing a gradual acceptance of new culinary habits. We don't talk about "exotic cuisine" anymore because exotic means faraway, strange, and not necessarily authentic. We no longer consider Chinese, Indian or Mexican food to be unusual fare. The sources of inspiration for our cooking no longer matter as long as the results are delicious. It used to be that trying our hand at foreign cuisine was considered audacious, daring, but today it's part of our everyday lives. Ingredients that, in the past, had to be tracked with the skill of a detective or brought back by travelling friends, are now available locally from the neighborhood supermarket or even our corner grocer. We are no longer intimidated by peculiar spices, mysterious jars, or colorful fruits—but instead—we are learning how to use them. The world is coming to us and its flavors are being awakened in our kitchens. At the same time, we're discovering different ways of eating as well as dietary principles and eating habits from other countries. Our kitchens have become the melting pot for a natural blending of tastes; what was once quite curious is now so familiar that we forget its origins are foreign.

Mexican cuisine is known mostly as Tex-Mex cooking; however, the differences between the two are not to be confused. North of the border, you find cooking with the barbecue and chili con carne. They are delicious, to be sure, but they have very little in common with the foreign and subtle flavors of the earthy and expertly seasoned dishes from Mexico. This cuisine as it existed before the Spanish conquest was only a little different from its current form: They used chocolate, chiles, beans, squash and corn, much like today. Pre-Columbian recipes have survived for centuries: Colorful and fragrant stews, tamales wrapped in corn husks and tortillas. Aztec and Mayan cuisines were light, balanced and refined. In its best form, Mexican cuisine has preserved that refinement. Peppers are used for their dietetic properties and their unique flavor, and tomatoes are in their native element; but their favorite herb, fresh cilantro (coriander), remains an enigma because it is not native to America and we do not know who introduced it, or when. At any rate, Mexican cuisine requires lots of love, a certain dexterity and a sense of proportion. Follow the recipes, and you will be able to reproduce the traditional elegance of the cuisine served at the Mexican table. The results, a thousand miles from the more casual cookery of the Tex-Mex region, will delight and surprise you.

contents

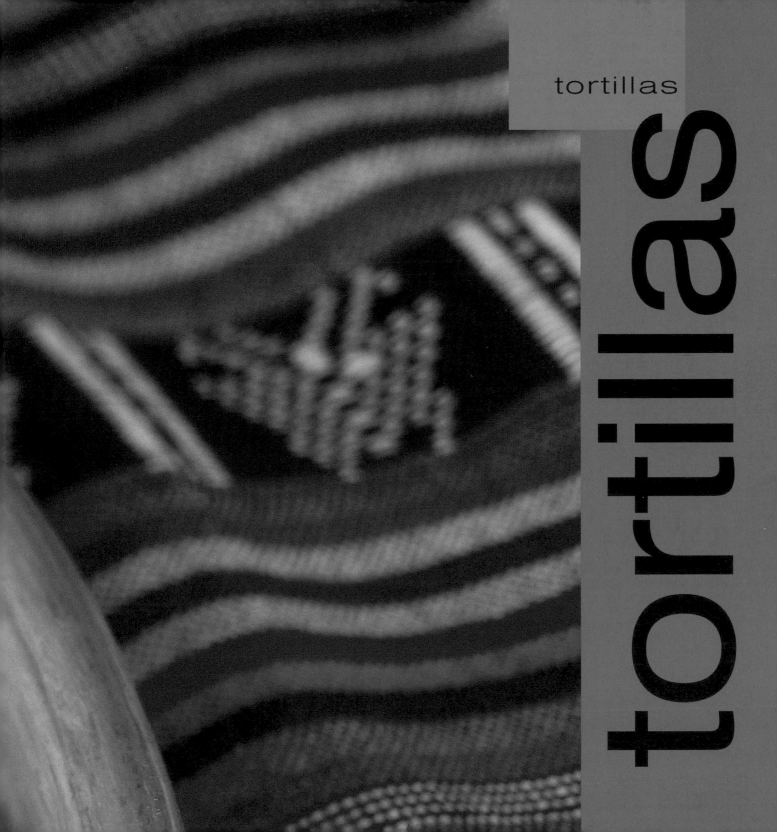

tortillas

tortillas

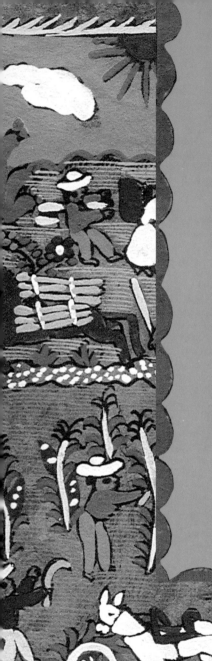

nourishing corn

The tortilla, a fine pancake cooked over a flat grill, serves as bread in Mexico and is the basis of multiple recipes. Its light, sour taste is due to the main ingredient, masa harina (corn flour) that can be found in specialty stores and most supermarkets. You can also find whole-wheat tortillas, as well as other more unusual ones made of blue corn. Well wrapped, all tortillas can be kept refrigerated or frozen.

[corn tortillas]

Makes 6 tortillas
Prep time: 20 minutes

1 cup masa harina
  (corn flour)
½ teaspoon salt

Mix the masa harina and salt and gradually add ½ cup plus 2 tablespoons warm water, stirring constantly until blended. Knead mixture with your hands until you get a uniform dough that doesn't stick to your fingers.

Divide the dough in 6 equal balls. Line a working surface with plastic wrap, place a ball in the center, cover it with plastic wrap and flatten it with a plate until the pancake measures about 6 inches in diameter.

Continue this method with all the dough balls. To shape them, you can also use a tortilla press.

Depending on the recipe, these tortillas can be precooked or kept separated by layers of wax paper and wrapped in plastic wrap.

[wheat tortillas stuffed with turkey]

Mix the flour, a pinch of salt and the baking powder. Gradually work in 2 tablespoons oil, then work in 2 tablespoons warm water and mix with the fingers until well-blended

On a floured surface, work the mixture with your hands until the dough is perfectly uniform. Roll it into a ball, wrap it in a warm, moist cloth and let it rest for 15 minutes in a warm place.

Divide the dough in four parts. On a floured working surface, flatten each one with your hands into a round about 4 inches in diameter. Using a rolling pin, stretch it to a pancake 8 inches in diameter.

Peel and cut the tomatoes, the onions and the avocado into small cubes to make a salsa.

Heat a dry frying pan and cook the tortillas, one at a time, over low heat for about 1 minute on one side and 45 seconds on the other.

Coarsely mash the red beans. Cut the turkey meat into small pieces, cook them for 10 minutes in ½ tablespoon of the oil and add some salt.

On each tortilla, layer some of the red beans, add some turkey and sliced cheese and fold it in two. In a very hot frying pan, heat the remaining 2 tablespoons of oil and cook the tortillas for 10 minutes, until they are golden brown. Drain them on paper towels and serve with the chopped vegetables.

Serves 4
Prep time: 30 minutes
Cooking time: 20 minutes
Resting time: 15 minutes

Prepare the tortillas:
½ cup whole-wheat flour, plus extra for flouring work surface
Salt
½ teaspoon baking powder
2 tablespoons oil

Prepare the filling:
2 tomatoes
1 onion
1 avocado
⅔ cup cooked red beans
½ pound white turkey meat
2½ tablespoons oil, divided
¼ pound cheddar or jack cheese, thinly sliced

[cheese turnovers]

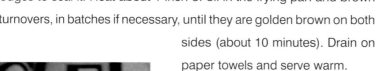

Peel and chop the garlic and onion. Plunge the tomato in boiling water for a few seconds. Peel and cut it in chunks. Wash and split the chile peppers in half lengthwise, remove the seeds and chop finely.

Brown the garlic and onion in the olive oil. When they become transparent stir in the flour and then the crème fraîche. Cook for 20 minutes over low heat. Stirring continuously, add the tomato and peppers.

Cut the cheeses in small chunks. Add them to the frying pan and stir until they are completely melted. The mixture must be smooth like a thick mayonnaise. Let it cool.

Distribute 2 tablespoons of filling on each tortilla, fold it in two and fold the edges to seal it. Heat about 1 inch of oil in the frying pan and brown the turnovers, in batches if necessary, until they are golden brown on both sides (about 10 minutes). Drain on paper towels and serve warm.

Serves 4
Prep time: 1 hour
Cooking time: 30 minutes

1 clove garlic
1 onion
1 large ripe tomato
2 fresh chile peppers
¼ cup olive oil
1 tablespoon wheat flour
⅔ cup crème fraîche
1½ pound various cheeses
  (cheddar, Monterey Jack,
  Swiss)
4 whole-wheat tortillas
  (see page 28)
Oil for frying

Serves 4
Prep time: 30 minutes
Cooking time: 15 minutes

1 clove garlic
¾ pound ground beef
1 tablespoon oil
Powdered cumin
Salt
1 red chile pepper
1 cup tomato sauce
Oil for frying
4 corn tortillas (see page 11)
¼ cup crème fraîche
Juice of 1 lemon
1 bunch fresh cilantro,
   chopped

[red cigars]

Peel and mince the garlic. Brown the ground beef and the garlic in oil, for 5 minutes. Sprinkle with some cumin and add salt to taste.

Wash the chile pepper, split in half lengthwise, remove the seeds, and slice it. Put the tomato sauce and the pepper in a saucepan, sprinkle with cumin and simmer for 15 minutes on low heat.

Preheat the oven to 350°F.

Heat enough oil to coat the bottom of a skillet and fry tortillas for a few seconds on each side, to soften. Drain them on paper towels. Put 1 tablespoon of filling on each tortilla and then roll it so that it resembles a cigar. Place the cigars on an ovenproof dish, spread the tomato sauce on top and bake them for 15 minutes in the oven at 350°F.

Just before serving, mix the crème fraîche with the lemon juice. Serve the sauce-covered cigars with the lemon crème fraîche on the side. Sprinkle with the chopped cilantro.

[chili sauce]

Makes 1¼ cups of sauce
Prep time: 15 minutes
Cooking time: 10 minutes

1 large ripe tomato
1 onion
1 clove garlic
½ green bell pepper
1 leek (white part only)
3 fresh green chiles
Salt
3 ounces bacon
2 tablespoons flour
½ teaspoon
   cayenne pepper
1 tablespoon vinegar

Peel and chop the tomato. Peel and chop the onion and garlic. Chop the bell pepper and leek. Wash the chiles, cut in half lengthwise, remove the seeds and chop finely. Mix all these vegetables together and season with salt.

Slice the bacon and cook it in a saucepan. Add the flour and, when it begins to turn golden brown, add the vegetables, cayenne pepper and the vinegar. Stir the sauce, while it cooks for 3 minutes. Serve cold.

[green sauce]

Peel and chop the onion and garlic. Wash the coriander, dry it thoroughly in paper towels and pull off the leaves. Wash the chile and the bell pepper, cut in half lengthwise, and remove seeds and chop.

Put all the ingredients for the sauce, except salt, in a food processor and process until you obtain a purée. Season with salt. Refrigerate for 1 hour, minimum. Serve chilled.

Makes 1½ cups sauce
Prep time: 10 minutes
Refrigeration time: 1 hour

1 white onion
1 clove garlic
½ bunch fresh coriander
1 small green chile pepper
½ sweet green bell pepper
4 tomatillos, canned
Salt

[buns with red beans]

Serves 4
Prep time: 30 minutes
Cooking time: 30 minutes
Resting time: 30 minutes

3⅓ cups masa harina
   (corn flour)
½ cup oil, plus
   2 tablespoons
Salt
3 tomatoes
3 small chile peppers
2 cloves garlic
1 onion
1 bunch fresh cilantro
9 ounces pureed red beans
   (or one 15-ounce can
   drained and puréed)
Oil for frying

Mix the masa harina with ⅓ cup water, the oil and 1 pinch of salt. Knead until it becomes a uniform dough. Let it rest for 30 minutes.

Drop the tomatoes in boiling water, cool and peel them. Wash chiles, cut in half lengthwise, and remove the seeds. Peel the garlic and onion.

Put all these ingredients in a food processor, add the cilantro and beans, and process until smooth. Reduce over low heat, for about 10 minutes. Add salt to taste.

Form balls of dough about the size of a ping pong ball. Make a hole with your index finger and fill it with some of the bean purée. Flatten them until they become thick medallions. Heat a large skillet, and add about 1 inch of oil and fry buns for 10 minutes on each side. Serve them covered with the warm sauce.

[fried tortilla roll-ups]

Warm the tortillas in a 300°F oven to soften them.

Cut the chicken breasts in small pieces. Peel and mince the onion. Heat 1 tablespoon of the olive oil in a pan and brown the chicken and the onion for 10 minutes. Add salt and pepper. Put one fourth of the chicken on one side of each tortilla, cover it with slices of cheese, roll it and fold up the ends of the tortilla. Hold them together with wooden toothpicks.

Heat a large skillet, and add the remaining olive oil and cook the roll-ups for 10 minutes, turning to cook evenly. Remove them when they are golden brown, drain them on paper towels and keep them warm in the oven.

Wash and drain the lettuce leaves and cut them in strips. Drop the tomato in boiling water, let it cool, peel it and cut it in chunks. Cut the avocado in half, remove the pit and the skin and cut the flesh in cubes. Crumble the feta over the tortilla roll-ups and serve them with some lettuce, tomato and avocado on the side.

Serves 4
Prep time: 30 minutes
Cooking time: 10 minutes

4 whole-wheat tortillas
2 chicken breasts
   (6 ounces each)
1 onion
3 tablespoons olive oil,
   divided
Salt and pepper
3 ounces cheddar or
   Monterey Jack cheese,
   thinly sliced
4 lettuce leaves
1 tomato
1 avocado
2 ounces feta cheese

[stuffed tacos]

Warm the taco shells in a 300°F oven.

Wash, drain and cut the lettuce in strips. Drain the corn. Wash the tomatoes and cut in thin slices. Cut the ham and the cheese in small strips. Cut the avocado in two, remove the pit, peel, and thinly slice the flesh.

Mix all the ingredients with the vinaigrette and fill the warm taco shells. Serve immediately.

Serves 4
Prep time: 20 minutes
Cooking time: 5 minutes

8 taco shells
1 head lettuce
1 small can sweet corn
   (11 ounces)
2 ripe tomatoes
4 ounces ham
4 ounces cheddar cheese
1 avocado
⅓ cup olive oil vinaigrette

While wonderful Mexican cheeses are now being made in the U.S. as well as south of the border, there are many acceptable substitutes. Cheddar, Monterey Jack, feta and Swiss (depending on the dish being made) can all enhance the delicious flavors of Mexican cooking.

[chicken turnovers]

Finely chop the chicken breast and brown it in a pan with peanut or olive oil. Season it with the soy sauce and a few drops of Tabasco. Let it cool completely before adding the cheese and the sour cream. Mix it well.

Place 2 tablespoons of the filling on each tortilla, fold it in two and fold the edges to seal it all together.

Heat about 1 inch of oil in a frying pan. When the oil is hot, fry the turnovers, two at a time, for 10 minutes on each side or until they are golden brown. Drain them on paper towels and serve them very warm.

Serves 4
Prep time: 30 minutes
Cooking time: 20 minutes

1 chicken breast
   (about 6 ounces)
2 tablespoons peanut
   or olive oil
½ tablespoon soy sauce
A few drops Tabasco sauce
¼ cup grated cheese
   (see above for types
   of cheeses)
1 tablespoon sour cream
   (or crème fraîche with a
   few drops of lemon juice)
4 whole-wheat tortillas
Oil for frying

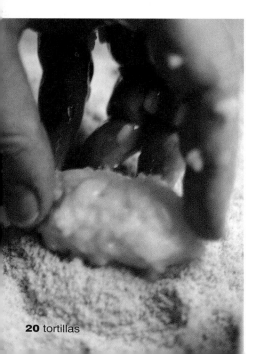

[green cigars]

Serves 4
Prep time: 30 minutes
Cooking time: 30 minutes

2 mild green chiles
1 clove garlic
2 onions
1 pound tomatillos
½ bunch fresh coriander
Salt
1 tablespoon oil, plus more for frying
¾ pound cooked chicken
¼ pound ground beef
1 teaspoon powdered cumin
Pepper
4 corn tortillas (see page 11)
¼ cup chicken broth
6 ounces grated cheese
(see page 20, top)
2 tablespoons crème
fraîche

To prepare the sauce: Wash the chile peppers, cut in half lengthwise and remove the seeds. Peel the garlic and onions. In a food processor, mix the tomatillos, garlic, coriander leaves, green chiles, half of an onion and a pinch of salt. Cook the mixture for 5 minutes in 1 tablespoon of oil. Set aside.

To prepare the filling: Chop the cooked chicken and the other half of the onion. Brown it for 5 minutes in a bit of oil, with the ground beef, seasoned with cumin, salt and pepper.

Preheat oven to 350°F.

Heat a skillet, add a small amount of oil, and cook the tortillas for a few seconds to soften them. Dip them, one at a time, in the sauce. Put some of the meat filling on each tortilla and roll to enclose filling. Arrange cigars on an ovenproof baking dish, cover them with some of the sauce (not all of it), pour the chicken broth over the top, sprinkle with grated cheese and the remaining onion (finely chopped). Put in the oven and cook for 30 minutes.

Serve with the rest of the sauce and the crème fraîche on the side.

[fried shells]

Knead the flour with salt and about ¼ cup warm water until you obtain a uniform dough. Shape dough into 18–20 balls about the size of a large walnut and then make a depression with the thumb. Heat the frying oil and when it is quite hot (350°F) drop the shells in the oil. Fry them for 2–3 minutes on each side. Drain them on paper towels and keep them warm in the oven.

Cut the chicken breast in small pieces. Heat 1 tablespoon of the oil in a pan and cook the chicken for about 10 minutes, until it gets golden brown.

Prepare the sauce: Drop the chile in boiling water for 5 minutes. Cut in half lengthwise and remove the seeds. Drain the tomatillos. Put all the ingredients for the sauce in the food processor and purée. Set aside.

Cook the tomatillo sauce for 5 minutes. Using a teaspoon, put some of the sauce into each shell. Arrange, open side up, on a large plate, and fill them with the fried chicken, chopped onion and cheese. Serve right away.

Serves 4
Prep time: 20 minutes
Cooking time: 15 minutes

⅔ cup masa harina
  (corn flour)
1 teaspoon salt
1¼ cups oil for frying
1 chicken breast
  (about 5 ounces)

For the tomatillo sauce:
1 ounce (or more)
  green chiles
¾ pound canned tomatillos
  (about 12 ounces)
2 tablespoons
  chopped onion
1 bunch fresh cilantro,
  coarsely chopped
1 clove garlic, peeled
  and coarsely chopped

½ cup chopped onion
½ cup crumbled
  feta cheese

Peel the garlic and onion, wash the leek and chop all three. Drop the tomato in boiling water for a few seconds and let it cool. Peel it, remove the seeds and cut the pulp in thin strips. Cut the chiles in half lengthwise, remove seeds and finely chop.

Mix all the vegetables and add salt and pepper. Let the sauce sit at room temperature for 30 minutes before using.

Makes 1¼ cups of sauce
Prep time: 10 minutes
Rest: 30 minutes

1 clove garlic
1 onion
1 leek (white part only)
1 large ripe tomato
3 fresh mild green chiles
Salt and pepper

[mexican sauce]

It is impossible to imagine Mexican cuisine without its variety of chiles, used for their heat, but especially their flavor. The best known is the jalapeño. The little serrano is similar but less fragrant. We call the chile from the Antilles the delicious and fiery habanero. The chipotle, with its smoky flavor, is suitable for slow cooking and the ancho, which is less hot, is best for making sauces.

The oils in the flesh and seeds of chile peppers can irritate your skin and eyes. So always wear gloves, or work under cold running water.

[wheat tortillas]

Warm the milk over low heat and keep it warm. In a bowl, mix 4 cups of the flour with the baking powder and the salt. Add the lard, or the oil, slowly, and knead with your fingers. When it is well-blended, add the milk a little at a time. Continue kneading the dough until it is uniform and shape into small balls, the size of a walnut.

On a floured surface, press them with the hand first. Then, with a rolling pin, make them into tortillas about 7 to 8 inches in diameter.

Dust each one with flour.

Heat a dry nonstick pan and, over low heat, cook each tortilla for 1 minute on one side and 45 seconds on the other.

These precooked tortillas, wrapped in plastic wrap, will keep refrigerated for up to 2 days.

Serves 4
Prep time: 10 minutes
Cooking time: 20 minutes

½ cup milk
4 cups wheat flour, plus extra for rolling and dusting tortillas
1 tablespoon baking powder
1 teaspoon salt
2 tablespoons lard or olive oil

[chorizo turnovers]

Scald and peel the tomato; cut it in small chunks. Peel and chop the onion and garlic as well as the white of the leek. Wash the chiles, cut in half lengthwise, remove seeds, and finely chop. Mix all these vegetables, add salt and pepper, and let them rest for 30 minutes.

Crumble the chorizo and brown it in a nonstick pan. Put it in a ceramic dish and cover it with the vegetables and the cheese. Toss to mix.

Distribute 2 tablespoons of this filling on each tortilla, fold it in half and carefully close the edges to make sure the turnover is sealed.

Heat about 1 inch of oil in a frying pan and gently cook the turnovers, in batches if necessary, for 30 minutes or until they are golden brown on both sides. Drain them on paper towels and serve them, cut in sections, as an entrée.

Serves 4
Prep time: 30 minutes
Cooking time: 15 minutes
Resting time: 30 minutes

1 large ripe tomato
1 onion
1 clove garlic
1 leek (white part only)
3 green chiles
Salt and pepper
6 ounces fresh chorizo
2 ounces mild cheddar, grated
4 wheat tortillas
Oil for frying

Serves 4
Prep time: 50 minutes
Cooking time: 1hour

1 pound boned and
  chopped chicken
8 banana leaves
1 pound masa harina
  (corn flour)
1 teaspoon baking powder
1 teaspoon salt
⅔ cup lard
⅔ cup tomatillo sauce
  or mole sauce

[stuffed
banana leaves]

Put the chopped chicken in 6 cups of cold water, bring to a boil, reduce heat and simmer for 30 minutes. Drain the meat and reserve the broth. Drop the banana leaves in boiling water for 5 minutes, to soften them. Drain them, cut off the ends and cut the leaves in rectangles about 10 x 15 inches.

Mix the masa harina with the baking powder and salt. Add the lard, cut in pieces, and mix with your fingers while adding some of the chicken broth, a little at a time, until the dough cleans the sides of the bowl. Knead it until you obtain a uniform dough. Cut it in 8 portions and put one portion in the center of each leaf. Spread it out and layer some of the chicken on top. Drizzle with 1 tablespoon of the tomatillo sauce. Fold the leaf, length-wise, three times. Fold the ends in order to make a packet. Steam them for 30 minutes and serve.

soups & salads

soups & salads

freshness and spiciness

Mexican salads are served as side dishes rather than as entrées. The sour flavor of citrus fruits, the subtle sweetness of fresh coriander and the creamy texture of the avocado lighten the heat of other dishes. Soups provide a good opportunity to test the Mexican flavors and colors; they must be served warm and well seasoned.

Serves 4
Prep time: 20 minutes
Refrigeration time: 1 hour

1 large orange
1 white grapefruit
1 pink grapefruit
1 firm apple
3 tablespoons lime juice
1 pinch table salt
1 small bunch
  fresh coriander

[citrus fruit salad]

Using a sharp, pointed knife peel the citrus fruits over a bowl to catch the juice, then slice them in rounds.

Wash and core the apple. Cut it in cubes.

Mix all the fruits and drizzle them with the lime juice. Add the salt.

Sprinkle finely chopped cilantro over the salad and serve it well chilled.

[black bean soup]

Put the black beans in a large pan of cold water and soak them overnight.

The next day, cook them with the bay leaf in 1 quart of water for about 1 hour and 10 minutes, covered, over low heat.

Peel and chop the onion and garlic. Cut the bacon in pieces and cook for 10 minutes in a nonstick pan. Add the onion and garlic to the bacon.

Peel and seed the tomato, and chop the pulp. Add these ingredients and the beef broth to the beans. Add salt and pepper and simmer for 15 minutes, covered.

Cut the tortillas in strips and fry them in the oil for 5 minutes. Serve the soup sprinkled with the tortillas, with the crème fraîche on the side.

Serves 4
Prep time: 25 minutes
Soaking time: 12 hours
Cooking time:
1 hour 45 minutes

8 ounces dried black beans
1 bay leaf
1 onion
1 clove garlic
2 ounces lean bacon
1 tomato
1 quart beef broth
Salt and pepper
2 corn tortillas
3 tablespoons oil
4 teaspoons crème fraîche

[orange and avocado salad]

Mince the onion. Peel the oranges with a knife and cut them in quarters. Cut the unpeeled cucumber in quarters, and the peeled avocado in quarters. Put oranges, cucumber and avocado in a salad bowl with the onion and stir.

Prepare a vinaigrette with the oil, vinegar, a few drops of Tabasco, salt and pepper. Pour over the salad and gently mix. Refrigerate for 30 minutes before serving.

Serves 4
Prep time: 15 minutes
Refrigeration time:
30 minutes

½ purple onion
3 oranges
1 small cucumber
1 large avocado
1 tablespoon olive oil
1 teaspoon vinegar
A few drops Tabasco sauce
Salt and pepper

[chicken soup with red peppers and garbanzo beans]

In a large pot, heat the broth to boiling. Add chicken, reduce heat, and cook for 30 minutes. Remove chicken from heat, reserving cooking broth. When chicken is cold, bone it and cut the meat in small cubes. Put the bell peppers under the oven broiler, for about 15 minutes, until they are black on all sides. Peel them and cut them in strips.

Peel the garlic and onion and chop. Chop the bacon. Peel the potatoes, grate one and cut the other one in chunks.

In a pan, heat the oil and brown the chopped garlic, onion and bacon for 10 minutes. Add the chicken, the potatoes and the bell pepper strips, and cook them over medium heat, for 10 minutes. Next, pour the tomato sauce and the reserved chicken broth. Cook it at a slow boil for 20 minutes. Add the garbanzo beans, rinsed in cold water. Stir, and add salt, pepper, the cumin and Tabasco. Cook the soup for about 15 minutes more.

Serves 4
Prep time: 30 minutes
Cooking time: 1 hour

1 quart chicken broth
1 chicken (2 pounds)
3 red bell peppers
1 clove garlic
1 onion
3 ounces lean bacon
2 potatoes
3 tablespoons oil
$\frac{2}{3}$ cup tomato sauce
1 can garbanzo beans, i.e. chick peas (15 ounces)
Salt and pepper
1 pinch cumin
A few drops Tabasco sauce

[potato salad]

Serves 4
Prep time: 20 minutes
Cooking time: 30 minutes

3 medium-sized potatoes
Salt
2 slices bacon
2 shallots
2 mild green chiles
½ red bell pepper
¼ cup chicken broth
⅓ cup butter
⅓ cup crème fraîche
Pepper
2 hard-cooked eggs
Fresh chives

Peel and dice the potatoes. Cook them in salted boiling water for about 20 minutes: They must remain firm. Keep them warm.

Fry the bacon in a dry pan until crisp, break it in pieces and set aside. Peel and slice the shallots and brown them, for 5 minutes, in the same pan you used to cook the bacon in. Set aside.

Wash the chiles, cut them in half lengthwise, discard the seeds and chop them. Cut the bell pepper in strips.

Warm the chicken broth in a saucepan, and add the butter and the cream and a little pepper. Cover the warm potatoes with the cream, stirring carefully. Add the shallots, bacon, hard-cooked eggs cut in quarters, chiles and the bell pepper. Mix and serve warm sprinkled with minced chives.

[cold cream of avocado]

Serves 4
Prep time: 25 minutes
Refrigeration time:
at least 2 hours

1 mild green chile
2 large ripe avocados
Salt and pepper
Juice of 1 lime
½ cup crème fraîche
1 quart chicken broth
1 pinch freshly
  grated nutmeg
1 bunch fresh cilantro

Wash the chile, and cut in half lengthwise and discard the seeds. Cut the avocados in two, remove the pit and take out the flesh.

Put avocado and chiles in a food processor with salt and pepper to taste, the lime juice, crème fraîche, chicken broth and nutmeg. Mix until the cream becomes smooth and uniform. Cover it with plastic wrap and refrigerate for at least 2 hours.

Serve the cream sprinkled with finely chopped cilantro.

[cabbage salad]

Cut the chile in half lengthwise discard the seeds, and cut into thin strips. Beat the cream with the lemon juice and vinegar until it is emulsified. Add salt and pepper and the chile.

Wash the cabbage and cut it into thin strips. Peel and slice the carrots in thin rounds. Mix all the vegetables with the cream, cover and let it marinate overnight in the refrigerator.

Serve chilled.

Serves 4
Prep time: 20 minutes
Marinating time: 12 hours

½ mild green chile
⅔ cup heavy cream
Juice of 2 lemons
2 tablespoons vinegar
Salt and pepper
½ head white cabbage
2 medium-sized carrots

[tomato salad with chiles]

Serves 4
Prep time: 20 minutes

1¼ pounds tomatoes
1 green chile
1 bunch fresh cilantro
Juice of 1 lime
3 tablespoons olive oil
Salt and freshly
   ground pepper
1 clove garlic, minced

Drop the tomatoes in boiling water for a few seconds. Cool them, peel them and remove the seeds. Cut the pulp in chunks. Wash the chile, cut it open lengthwise, discard the seeds and cut it into thin strips. Rinse and dry the cilantro, pull off the leaves and coarsely chop.

Mix the chopped cilantro with the chile and tomatoes. Prepare a vinaigrette with the lime juice and olive oil, and salt and pepper. Pour it over the tomato salad and serve sprinkled with the minced garlic.

[carrot and grapefruit salad]

Serves 4
Prep time: 15 minutes
Cooking time: 30 minutes
Refrigeration time: 1 hour

1 grapefruit
3 tablespoons
   powdered sugar
1 medium-sized
   red cabbage
Salt
2 pounds carrots
½ cup raisins
Ground cinnamon

Remove the grapefruit peel and cut the flesh in cubes. Put it in a saucepan with the sugar and cook, over low heat, for 15 minutes. Drain the grapefruit and reserve the liquid.

Remove the core and the thick outer leaves of the cabbage and cut it in big sections. Cook it for 15 minutes in salted water. Drain it well and cut it in thin strips. Let it cool.

Peel and grate the carrots. Mix them with the grapefruit and the cabbage, the reserved cooking liquid and the raisins. Sprinkle with cinnamon and serve very cold.

[guacamole]

Serves 4
Prep time: 20 minutes
Refrigeration time: 1 hour

⅓ cup chopped onions
1 bunch fresh cilantro
½ pound tomatoes
2 avocados
1 teaspoon salt
Juice of ½ lemon

Peel the onions and chop them. Rinse and dry the cilantro. Pull off the leaves and chop them finely. Drop the tomatoes in boiling water for a few seconds, peel and seed them. Cut them in chunks. Cut the avocados in half, remove the pit, take out the flesh and mash it with a fork.

Put together in a bowl, the mashed avocados, cilantro, onions, tomatoes, salt and the lemon juice. Stir and serve cold.

For true Mexican taste, use one to two cans of jalapeño chiles to flavor the Tortilla Soup (see this page). You can remove the seeds, if you don't want it too spicy.

[tortilla soup]

Serves 4
Prep time: 20 minutes
Cooking time 10 minutes

8 corn tortillas
  (see page 11)
2 tablespoons oil
1 red chile pepper
4 tomatoes
2 cloves garlic
1 onion
2 cups chicken broth
1 teaspoon dried
  lemon grass
⅓ cup crumbled feta
  cheese (about 3 ounces)
1 ripe avocado

Cut the tortillas in wide strips, ¼ inch long, and cook them for 5 minutes in the oil. When they are golden brown, lift them out of the pan, reserving the cooking oil, and drain them on paper towels.

Wash, cut open the chile lengthwise and remove the seeds. Brown the chile for 5 minutes in the same pan and using the oil used for the tortillas.

Lift from the pan, reserving the remaining oil. Scald the tomatoes in boiling water and cool. Peel tomatoes, garlic and onion and coarsely chop. Process the tomatoes, garlic and onion in a food processor until smooth. Reduce the sauce, in the reserved oil, for 15 minutes. Add the chicken broth, the tortilla strips, chile and lemon grass. Bring it to a boil.

Cube the feta cheese and the avocado and serve them, on the side, with the hot soup.

[red bean soup]

Serves 4
Prep time: 30 minutes
Cooking time: 1 hour

1 clove garlic
1 onion
Olive oil
2 ounces lean bacon
2 carrots
1 potato
¾ pound chorizo, sliced
⅔ cup tomato sauce
1 quart chicken broth
15 ounces canned red beans
Salt and pepper
1 pinch cumin
A few drops Tabasco sauce

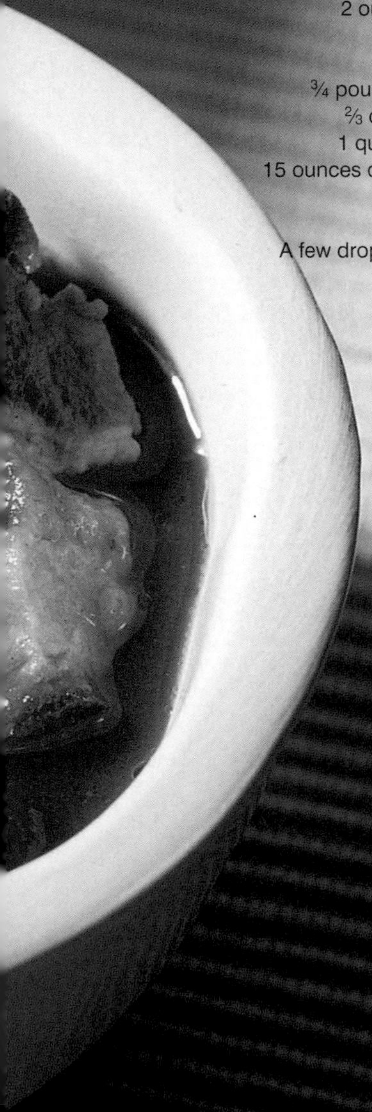

Peel the garlic and onion and chop them. Brown them in 1 tablespoon of olive oil. Cut the bacon in pieces.

Peel and cube the carrots and the potato. In a large pot, brown the bacon in 3 tablespoons of olive oil, for 10 minutes. Add the carrots and potato, the sliced chorizo and mix well. Cook on low heat for 30 minutes.

Add the tomato sauce and the chicken broth, and bring it to a boil. Lower the heat and cook slowly for 20 minutes. Next, add the chopped garlic and onion, the red beans and mix them. Add salt and pepper, the cumin and a few drops of Tabasco.

Simmer for 15 minutes and serve very warm.

[corn soup]

Bring 1 quart of salted water to a boil. Drop in the ears of corn and cook them for 1 hour. When they are cold, cut off the kernels, reserving 2 tablespoons for garnish. In a food processor, process the rest of the corn with some of its own cooking liquid and half of the evaporated milk until fairly smooth.

Melt the butter in a pan, put in the creamed corn, and pour the rest of the milk and ⅔ cup of the cooking liquid from the corn. Season with salt and pepper, and add the reserved kernels and the chile pepper. Cook for 10 minutes on low heat.

Serve warm with small bread croutons fried in olive oil.

Serves 4
Prep time: 20 minutes
Cooking time:
1 hour 15 minutes

Salt
4 ears of corn
1 can evaporated milk
  (12 ounces)
1½ tablespoons butter
Salt and pepper
1 chile pepper
Croutons fried in olive oil

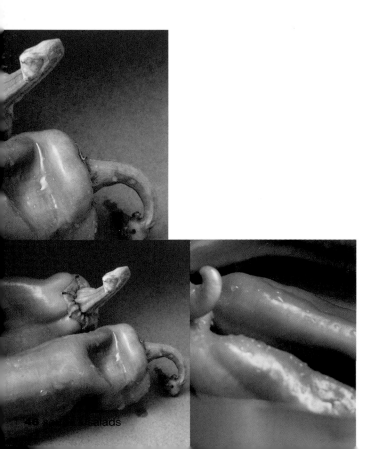

[mexican salad]

Peel and dice the avocados and immediately drizzle them with the lemon juice to keep them from turning brown.

Wash the chiles, cut in half lengthwise, discard seeds and chop them finely. Chop the onion and the cilantro. Put all the ingredients in a salad bowl, add salt, and drizzle with olive oil and toss.

Serve the salad as an accompaniment to grilled meat or recipes that call for tortillas.

Serves 4
Prep time: 10 minutes

3 avocados
Juice of 1 lemon
2 small green chiles
½ onion
1 bunch fresh cilantro
Salt
4 tablespoons olive oil

[tomato soup]

Serves 4
Prep time: 20 minutes
Refrigeration time: 2 hours

In a bowl, mix the tomato juice, olive oil and vinegar. Scald the tomato, cool it, peel it and remove the seeds. Cut the ends of the cucumber. Peel and crush the garlic. Wash and seed the pepper. **D**ice all these vegetables, as well as the celery and onion, before adding them to the bowl. Mix well and add salt and pepper.

Refrigerate for 2 hours and serve very cold topped with the fried croutons and a sprinkle of chopped parsley.

1 quart tomato juice
3 tablespoons olive oil
2 tablespoons light vinegar
1 tomato
1 small cucumber
1 clove garlic
1 green bell pepper
1 rib celery
½ onion
Salt and pepper
Croutons fried in olive oil
2 tablespoons chopped
  fresh parsley

Serves 4
Prep time: 10 minutes

1 can of nopales
  (cooked cactus)
3 tablespoons vinegar
3 tablespoons oil
Salt and pepper
2 tomatoes
1 onion
⅓ cup crumbled feta
  cheese (about 3 ounces)
1 tablespoon dried oregano

[cactus salad]

Drain the nopales.

Prepare the vinaigrette mixing the vinegar, oil, salt and pepper. Wash the tomatoes, peel the onion and slice them in rounds. Place the cactus, tomatoes and onions in a salad bowl. Pour the vinaigrette over them, add the crumbled cheese, sprinkle the oregano and add salt to taste.

Serve the salad alone or use it to accompany dishes made with tortillas.

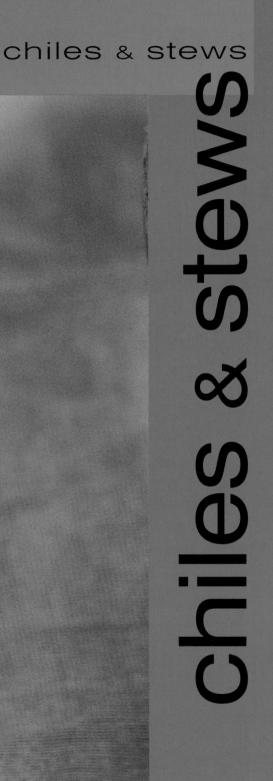

chiles & stews

chiles & stews

chile peppers and chocolate

Mexican sauces, inherited from Pre-Columbian cuisine, are complex and flavorful. Meats and fowl are simmered in them, the most popular being pork. The famous mole poblano, a turkey or chicken stew, is a very old mixture of spices and bitter chocolate. The well-known chili con carne, on the other hand, is really a Texan recipe included here due to its popularity in Mexican restaurants.

Serves 4
Prep time: 30 minutes
Cooking time: 10 minutes

3 dried chipotle
   chile peppers
5 tomatoes,
   coarsely chopped
4 cloves garlic
¾ teaspoon cumin, divided
1 teaspoon ground oregano
1¼ pound ground beef
2 eggs
½ cup bread crumbs
Salt and pepper
2 tablespoons olive oil

[beef croquettes]

Put the peppers in a bowl with warm water and soak them for 5 minutes. Cut in half lengthwise and remove the seeds. Process chiles with the tomatoes, 2 peeled garlic cloves, ¼ teaspoon of the cumin and oregano. Put this sauce through a strainer and then reduce it for 15 minutes over low heat.

Mix the ground beef with the remaining cumin, and 2 peeled and minced garlic cloves, the beaten eggs, bread crumbs, salt and pepper.

Shape the croquettes about the size of a walnut. Heat the oil in a skillet and fry croquettes for 10 minutes. Serve them warm, covered with the sauce.

[rabbit in wraps]

Scald the tomatoes, peel them and cut them in chunks. Peel and chop the onions. Peel and crush the garlic. Cut the rabbit in 8 pieces and sprinkle with salt.

Heat the oil in a pan and fry the onions and garlic until they are transparent. Add the tomatoes and cook, over low heat, for 4 to 5 minutes.

Add the tomato concentrate, coarsely chopped olives, the bell pepper cut in small pieces, chopped parsley, and salt and pepper to taste. Cook for 5 to 10 minutes.

Cut 8 pieces of aluminum foil and put, in each one, one piece of rabbit completely covered with the sauce, and close the package well to seal the edges. Steam the 8 packets for 1 hour and serve them very warm.

Serves 4
Prep time: 25 minutes
Cooking time:
1 hour 15 minutes

1 pound tomatoes
¼ pound onions
2 cloves garlic
1 rabbit (3 pounds)
Salt
2 tablespoons oil
1 small can tomato
    concentrate
¼ cup pitted black olives
    (about 2 ounces)
3 tablespoons canned
    red bell peppers
1 tablespoon chopped
    fresh parsley
Pepper

[pork stew with white corn]

Wash the radishes and cut off the tops. Cut the meat in pieces. Peel the white onion and stick the cloves in it. Peel and crush the garlic. In a large pot, bring to a boil 2 quarts of water. Add the pork meat, the onion with the cloves, the garlic, beef bouillon, chili powder and the bouquet garni. **C**over and simmer for 2½ hours, skimming the liquid often.

Drain and rinse the corn, add it to the pot and simmer for another 10 minutes over low heat. Add salt and pepper to taste.

In the meantime, wash the cabbage and chop it finely, and finely chop the radishes. Peel the red onion and slice it thinly. Brush the lime under cold water and then quarter it.

Serve the pork stew, nice and hot, and the cabbage, red onion, radishes, lime, oregano, and Tabasco in small bowls as accompaniments.

Serves 4
Prep time: 20 minutes
Cooking time: 3 hours

4 radishes
1 pound boneless pork
  shoulder
1 large white onion
2 cloves
1 clove garlic
½ cube beef bouillon
1 tablespoon chili powder
1 bouquet garni
  (1 bay leaf, parsley stalks
  and 1 sprig fresh thyme;
  tied together with string)
1 large can white corn
  (15 ounces)
Salt and pepper
½ pound white cabbage
1 small red onion
1 lime
2 tablespoons
  dried oregano
Tabasco sauce

[pork with black beans]

Serves 4
Prep time: 25 minutes
Soaking time: 12 hours
Cooking time: 25 minutes

10 ounces dried
  black beans
2 white onions
4 cloves garlic
2 pounds pork meat
½ teaspoon salt
4 tablespoons oil
2 tablespoons dried
  epazote or lemon grass
1 bunch radishes
1 red onion
2 limes
2 tablespoons
  ground oregano
2 tablespoons chili powder

Put the black beans in 1 quart of cold water and soak them overnight. Next day, peel the white onions and the garlic cloves.

Cut the meat in pieces and sprinkle with the salt. Heat the oil in a stew pot and, when it is very hot, brown the meat for 10 minutes. Then, add the beans with their soaking water, the whole white onions, garlic cloves and epazote. Cover and cook for 2½ hours.

During that time, wash the radishes, cut off the ends and slice them. Peel and chop the red onion. Brush the limes under cool water and slice them in thin rounds.

Serve the pork and the black beans with the lime slices, oregano, chopped red onion, radishes and chili powder and set in small bowls.

[mashed potatoes with chile pepper]

Serves 4
Prep time: 30 minutes
Cooking time: 15 minutes

2 dried guajillo
  chile peppers
2 tablespoons oil
¼ cup chicken broth
3 medium-sized potatoes
Salt
3 cloves garlic
3 tablespoons butter
⅓ cup whole milk
Salt

Wash and cut the peppers in half lengthwise and discard the seeds. Heat the oil in a pan and brown the peppers, over medium-high heat, for 5 minutes. Process the chile peppers and chicken broth in a food processor until blended.

Peel the potatoes and cook them in salted water for about 30 minutes. Grill the unpeeled garlic cloves in a dry pan for 10 minutes. Mix the garlic pulp, the butter and the milk with the pepper purée.

Drain the potatoes, mash them with a fork and add them to the preceding mixture. Mix to combine and serve warm.

[stuffed bell peppers with cheese]

Preheat the oven broiler. Put the bell peppers on the middle rack and cook them for 15 minutes until the skin blisters on all sides. Peel them and take out the seeds and fill each pepper with a slice of cheese. Dust them with flour.

Break the eggs, separating the whites from the yolks. Beat the whites until firm and gently fold the yolks into the whites. Add a pinch of flour, salt and pepper. Cover the bell peppers with the egg mixture and fry them, in oil, for about 8 minutes. Drain them on paper towels.

Process the tomato sauce in a food processor with the garlic and onion. Pour it in a saucepan and add salt, pepper, the bay leaf and sugar.

Bring the sauce to a boil, spread it over the bell peppers and serve right away.

Serves 4
Prep time: 40 minutes
Cooking time: 8 minutes

4 green bell peppers
½ pound cheese, cut in
  4 slices (to fit in peppers)
Flour
3 eggs
Salt and pepper
1¼ cups oil
16 ounces tomato sauce
1 peeled clove garlic
3 tablespoons chopped onion
1 bay leaf
1 teaspoon sugar

[corn fritters]

Serves 4
Prep time: 20 minutes
Cooking time: 15 minutes

20 ounces canned
  sweet corn
1 cup whole-wheat flour
1 pinch baking powder
2 eggs
2 tablespoons
  bread crumbs
4 ounces canned,
  chopped green chiles
1 pinch salt
2 tablespoons oil

Drain the corn. Put all ingredients (except oil) into a food processor and process until combined (be careful not to over mix).

Heat the oil in a large skillet until it is very hot. Drop the dough, by tablespoons, making sure that they do not touch. Fry them for 8 minutes, until they are golden brown on all sides. Drain the fritters on paper towels.

Continue with all the fritters and serve them immediately.

[turkey with chocolate]

Serves 4
Prep time: 20 minutes
Cooking time: 1 hour

2 onions
2 cloves garlic
1 pound turkey pieces
1 teaspoon salt, plus
  additional for water
2/3 cup mole sauce
2 tablespoons oil
2 ounces bittersweet
  chocolate, coarsely
  chopped
1 teaspoon brown sugar
3/4 cup rice
Sesame seeds

Peel and mince the onions. Peel the garlic. Bone all the turkey pieces and place them in a pot with 1½ cups water, half of the onion, 1 of the garlic cloves and 1 teaspoon of salt. Simmer for 40 minutes.

Into the bowl of a food processor put the mole sauce, ⅓ cup of the broth from cooking the turkey, the rest of the onions and the other garlic clove. Mix until the sauce is uniform.

Heat a large skillet, add oil and fry the sauce in hot oil, for 10 minutes, with ¼ cup of the broth from cooking the turkey, the dark chocolate and the sugar. Cook it on low heat for 20–25 minutes, stirring, until the sauce becomes very thick. Add the turkey pieces, turning them until they are all covered with the sauce, and cook them for another 10 minutes.

Cook the rice in salted, boiling water for 20 minutes and then drain it. Toast the sesame seeds, for 5 minutes, in a dry pan and sprinkle them over the rice. Serve immediately with the turkey.

[grilled lamb chops]

Serves 4
Prep time: 10 minutes
Cooking time: 10 minutes
Marinating time: 1 hour

2 lemons
1 clove garlic
2 tablespoons oil
3 tablespoons soy sauce
3/4 cup sherry
2 dried red chiles
1 teaspoon dried oregano
2 tablespoons ketchup
1 teaspoon Tabasco sauce
1/2 teaspoon salt
8 lamb chops

Squeeze the lemons over a bowl to obtain the juice. Peel the garlic and put it in the food processor with the lemon juice, oil, and all the remaining ingredients, except lamb chops. Mix well.

Put the chops in a dish with sides and cover them with the sauce. Put them in the refrigerator to marinate, for 1 hour, turning them over from time to time.

Cook the chops on a hot grill, for about 10 minutes, turning them twice and basting them often with the marinade.

In Central America, the chorizo, legacy of the conquistadores, is milder than its Spanish equivalents. It flavors soups and stews. If you can find it, use it with this chicken dish.

[chicken with chorizo]

Serves 4
Prep time: 30 minutes
Cooking time: 55 minutes

1 cleaned chicken
   (4 pounds)
3 tablespoons olive oil
10 ounces chorizo
2 onions
1 clove garlic
2 large ripe tomatoes
2 fresh chiles
1 tablespoon chopped
   fresh cilantro
Salt and pepper
¼ cup red wine
1 tablespoon vinegar

Cut the chicken in pieces. In a large nonstick skillet, brown the chicken in hot olive oil for 10 minutes, until the pieces are golden brown. Remove them and keep them warm.

In the same oil, cook the chorizo. Remove it and keep it warm also.

Peel and mince the onions. Peel and chop the garlic. Scald the tomatoes for a few seconds in a pan of boiling water and, when they cool off, peel and chop them. Wash the chiles, cut in half lengthwise, remove the seeds, and chop them.

In the drippings from the chorizo, on low heat, brown the onion and garlic for 15 minutes. Add the tomatoes, cilantro and chopped chiles. Season with salt and pepper. Mix together well and then add the wine and vinegar. Bring it to a boil and simmer for 15–20 minutes, stirring until the sauce thickens.

Slice the chorizo in rounds, 1 inch thick, and put them in the sauce. Add the chicken pieces, cover and simmer, over low heat, for 20 minutes.

[mexican rice]

Serves 4
Prep time: 15 minutes
Cooking time: 35 minutes

2 large ripe tomatoes
1 clove garlic
1 red onion
1 tablespoon olive oil
⅔ cup beef broth
¾ cup long-grain rice
Salt and freshly ground pepper

Scald the tomatoes for a few seconds, peel them and seed them. Chop the flesh in chunks.

Peel and chop the garlic and onion and brown in a skillet in hot olive oil, for 15 minutes. Bring the broth to a boil in a saucepan. Add rice and cook for 10 minutes. Add the tomatoes and cook for 10 minutes longer. Add the onions and the garlic. Mix well, add salt and pepper, and serve immediately.

Rice is the ideal accompaniment for all beef and chicken stews.

[chili con carne]

Put the dried beans in a pan of cold water and soak them for 12 hours. Next day, drain them and put them in a saucepan with 1quart of water, and add the bouquet garni and cloves. Cook for 1 hour and then add some salt. Cook for 15 minutes longer and then drain the beans.

Peel and chop the garlic and onions. Scald the tomatoes for a few seconds in boiling water. Cool them, peel them and cut them in quarters. Wash the bell pepper, cut off the top and discard the seeds, and cut into strips.

In a large heavy pan, cook the meat for 5 minutes on high heat. Add the chopped garlic and onion and cook for another 10 minutes, stirring often. Add salt, pepper, tomatoes, bell pepper, tomato concentrate, and sprinkle with cumin, chili powder and oregano. Add the beans and ½ cup of water, stir, cover and simmer for 30 minutes over low heat.

To save the soaking and cooking time of the beans, you can substitute canned beans.

Serves 4
Prep time: 20 minutes
Soaking time: 12 hours
Cooking time: 2 hours

¾ cup dried red beans
1 bouquet garni
    (1 bay leaf, parsley stalks
    and 1 sprig fresh thyme;
    tied together with string)
3 cloves
Salt
3 cloves garlic
2 onions
2 tomatoes
1 green bell pepper
1 pound ground beef
Pepper
1 small can tomato
    concentrate
1 teaspoon
    powdered cumin
1 teaspoon hot chili
    powder (more or less
    according to taste)
½ teaspoon dried oregano

Cut the chicken in half, lengthwise, and then flatten the two halves by hand on a cutting board.

In a large dish, mix the olive oil, the jalapeño pepper sauce, red chili powder, salt and pepper. Coat both sides of the chicken halves with the sauce and marinate them in the refrigerator for 2 hours.

Preheat the oven to 425°F. Put the chicken halves in a baking dish and bake it for about 1 hour, turning it over after 30 minutes. Baste the chicken with the marinade several times. Serve very warm.

Serves 4
Prep time: 30 minutes
Marinating time: 2 hours
Cooking time: 1 hour

1 cleaned chicken
   (3 pounds)
¼ cup olive oil
¾ cup jalapeño
   pepper sauce
1 tablespoon red
   chili powder
Salt and pepper

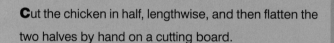

[baked chicken]

Marinades play a significant role in the cuisine of Latin

America. They are used to tenderize and season meats and

fowl. The jalapeño pepper lends its elegant fragrance to

the following recipe; you could also marinate chicken

wings for a few hours and cook them on a grill. The

habanero chile, in a small quantity and finely chopped,

gives grilled fowl a distinct flavor for a spicier variation.

[chiles with cheese]

Cube the cheese. Drain the peppers and peel the garlic. Mince the onion.

In a thick bottom pan, brown the onion in oil for 10 minutes. When it becomes transparent, add the green chiles, crushed garlic and then the cheese and the beer. Cook on low heat for 10 minutes, stirring constantly.

Warm the tortilla chips for 2 minutes in a 300°F oven. Serve the cheese dip in a fondue pot, with the tortilla chips on the side. Dip the tortilla chips in the warm, melted cheese.

Serves 4
Prep time: 30 minutes
Cooking time: 10 minutes

10 ounces cheddar cheese
1 can diced mild chile
   peppers (7 ounces)
1 clove garlic
½ onion
2 tablespoons oil
¼ cup beer
8 ounces tortilla chips

[summer squash with pork]

Cut the pork roast in pieces. Peel the onions and garlic. In a large pot, bring 1 quart of salted water to a boil and put in the meat with 1 quarter of the onion and 1 of the garlic cloves. When it returns to boil, lower the heat and cook for 40 minutes. Remove the meat and reserve the broth.

Wash the bell peppers, remove the seeds and cut in strips. Scald the tomatoes and let them cool. Peel them and put them through a food processor. Chop the rest of the onions and crush the other garlic clove.

Heat the olive oil in a skillet and fry the pieces of pork, for 10 minutes, with the onion, garlic and bell pepper strips. Add the tomatoes, tomato concentrate, salt and pepper, and cook for 30 minutes on low heat.

Dice the squash without peeling them, add them to the pan and cook for 30 minutes longer.

Sprinkle with the chopped cilantro and serve with fresh cream on the side.

Serves 4
Prep time: 30 minutes
Cooking time:
1 hour 20 minutes

1½ pounds boneless
   pork roast
2 onions
2 cloves garlic
Salt
6 ounces green
   bell peppers
3 tomatoes
2 tablespoons olive oil
¼ cup tomato concentrate
Pepper
3 summer squashes
   (zucchini, pattypan
   squash, etc.)
3 tablespoons chopped
   fresh cilantro
⅓ cup heavy cream

Serves 4
Prep time: 15 minutes
Cooking time:
1 hour 30 minutes

1 boned pork shoulder
1 large onion
1 tablespoon coriander
1 teaspoon
   powdered cumin
1 teaspoon
   powdered oregano
Salt
2 dried chiles
2 bay leaves
1¼ cups beef broth

[pork roast]

Put the meat in a stew pot with the peeled onion cut in quarters, coriander, cumin, oregano, some salt, the chiles, bay leaves, and broth. Cover and let it come to a boil slowly. Simmer for 1 hour over low heat, turning the meat over from time to time.

Preheat the oven to 500°F. Remove the meat and put it on a roasting pan. Cook it for 30 minutes on the middle rack in the preheated oven.

In the meantime, reduce the meat cooking liquid in half, over high heat, and then strain it. Slice the meat and bring it to the table with the sauce on the side. This dish can be served with potatoes, sautéed vegetables or mashed potatoes with chiles (see page 57).

fish

abundant and varied

Mexico, caressed by two oceans, enjoys an extraordinary variety of fish

and seafood. The large crawfish of the Gulf of Mexico are part of the cuisine

of Central America. Some species are not as well known, such as the

huachinango, which is traditionally cooked "a la Veracruz." As for ceviche, it is

a refined preparation of raw fish that is "cooked" in lime juice.

[fried shrimp]

Serves 4
Prep time: 10 minutes
Cooking time: 15 minutes

1½ pounds large raw shrimp
2 dried guajillo chiles
8 cloves garlic
3 tablespoons olive oil
1 tablespoon butter
Salt and pepper
½ bunch fresh coriander

Rinse and dry the shrimp. Wash the chiles, cut them in half lengthwise and remove the seeds. Cut the chiles in thin strips. Peel the garlic and cut it in thin strips.

In a large skillet, heat the oil and the butter and sauté the chiles and the garlic, over low heat, until they are a golden color. Add the shrimp and cook for 10 minutes over high heat. Add salt and pepper.

Serve sprinkled with chopped cilantro.

[flounder a la veracruz]

Rinse the fish fillets, put them on a plate and sprinkle with salt and pepper. Cover them with the lemon juice and marinate in the refrigerator for 1 hour. **P**eel and mince the onion. Peel and crush the garlic. In a large skillet, heat the oil and brown the onion and garlic for 15 minutes. Transfer them to a pan and add the court-bouillon, parsley sprigs, bay leaf and cinnamon stick all tied together. Cook for 10 minutes, and then add the olives, cloves, chile pepper, capers and juice from chiles. Simmer for 15 minutes. **S**cald the tomatoes, peel them, discard the seeds and chop the pulp. Remove the aromatic bouquet and strain the court-bouillon. Reheat it in a large skillet before adding the drained fish fillets and the tomatoes. Cover and cook, on medium heat, for 4 minutes. Turn the fillets over and cook for 4 minutes on the other side. Serve sprinkled with chopped parsley.

Serves 4
Prep time: 20 minutes
Cooking time: 40 minutes
Marinating time: 1 hour

4 flounder fillets
  (5 ounces each)
Salt and pepper
2 tablespoons lemon juice
1 onion
2 cloves garlic
3 tablespoons oil
⅔ cup court-bouillon (see
  page 82) or fish broth
½ bunch fresh parsley
1 bay leaf
1 small cinnamon stick
10 green olives, chopped
2 cloves
1 canned jalapeño
  chile, finely chopped
  (reserve juice)
2 tablespoons capers
1 tablespoon juice from
  the canned chiles
3 tomatoes

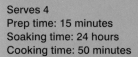

[cod tampico]

Put the cod in a deep pan with cold water and soak it for 24 hours, changing the water several times to get rid of the salt.

Next day, drain and rinse the cod and put it in a pan. Cover with cold water, bring it to a boil and then cook it for 10 minutes at a slow boil.

Preheat the oven broiler. Put the bell peppers on the middle rack and turn until the skin blisters all around. Peel the bell peppers, cut them in half, remove the top and the seeds, and cut the flesh in strips.

Peel and chop the onion and garlic. Wash the chiles, cut them open to discard the seeds and then slice them in rounds. In a skillet, sauté the onion in oil, on low heat, for 15 minutes until it becomes transparent. Add the garlic, then the bell peppers and the chiles, pour in ⅓ cup of water, and bring it to a boil. Simmer for 5 minutes, then blend the sauce in a food processor until smooth.

Drain the cod and cut it in pieces. Bring the sauce to a boil, add salt and pepper, and add the cod to the warm sauce. Cook the cod slowly over low heat, for 6–8 minutes and serve immediately.

Serves 4
Prep time: 15 minutes
Soaking time: 24 hours
Cooking time: 50 minutes

1½ pounds salt cod
3 medium-sized
  red bell peppers
1 large onion
6 cloves garlic
2 hot red chiles
2 tablespoons olive oil
Salt and pepper

[fried octopus]

Serves 4
Prep time: 10 minutes
Cooking time: 1 hour

3½ pounds octopus
⅓ cup white wine
1 onion
Salt
1 sprig fresh thyme
1 sprig fresh rosemary
2 fresh bay leaves
2 cloves
8 peppercorns
1 bunch fresh
   parsley, divided
1 head garlic
3 tablespoons butter
Juice of 1 lemon

Clean the octopus or ask your fish vendor to do it. Rinse them and put them in a pan with 1½ quarts of water, the white wine, the onion peeled and chopped coarsely, salt, thyme, rosemary, bay leaves, cloves, peppercorns and 5 sprigs from the bunch of parsley. Bring to a boil and cook for 1 hour over low heat. Let cool.

Peel and chop the garlic. Drain the octopus, peel and cut it into pieces. In a large skillet, cook the octopus and garlic in hot butter for 5 minutes, stirring constantly. Drizzle with the lemon juice, chop the rest of the parsley and add, and cook for 1 minute longer. Adjust the seasoning and serve immediately.

[baked chayote]

Serves 4
Prep time: 10 minutes
Cooking time: 55 minutes

3 large chayotes (mirliton)
Salt
6 ounces grated cheese
   (see page 20, top)
½ chopped onion
Pepper
Butter to grease baking dish
3 tablespoons bread crumbs
1 pinch sugar
1 pinch ground cinnamon
2 tablespoons butter,
   cut in pieces

Cook the chayotes with their skin on, in a large pot of salted, boiling water for 40 minutes. Drain them and cut them in half, lengthwise, being careful not to damage the skin. Using a spoon, scoop out the pulp, chop it and mix it with the cheese and the onion. Add salt and pepper.

Preheat the oven to 400°F. Fill the empty skins with the flesh and cheese mixture, and set them on a buttered baking dish. Sprinkle with the bread crumbs, sugar and cinnamon, and top with a few pieces of butter. Bake for 15 minutes.

[avocado with crab]

Peel and chop the shallots, and sauté them in olive oil in a heated skillet for 5 minutes. Remove from heat and add the crab meat, lime juice and mix until all the ingredients are warm. Set aside.

Cut the avocados in half, remove the pit, and scoop out the flesh with a spoon. Mash the avocado with the crème fraîche, cayenne pepper, paprika and some salt. Put a layer of avocado on a plate, add a layer of crab, and then another layer of avocado. Refrigerate for 30 minutes and serve cold.

Serves 4
Prep time: 15 minutes
Refrigeration time: 30 minutes

2 shallots
1 tablespoon olive oil
3 ounces canned crab meat
Juice of 1 lime
2 ripe avocados
¼ cup crème fraîche
1 pinch cayenne pepper
1 teaspoon paprika
Salt

Serves 4
Prep and cooking time:
about 50 minutes

1 pound potatoes
2 egg yolks
2 tablespoons
  grated cheese
  (see page 20, top)
Salt and pepper
Flour
Frying oil

[potato medallions]

Peel the potatoes and cook them in a steamer for 30 minutes. Purée them, and add the egg yolks, grated cheese, salt and pepper.

With moist hands, shape compact medallions about 2 inches thick and 3 inches in diameter. Flour them on both sides and fry them in hot oil in a skillet for 4 minutes on each side.

Serve them warm with flounder a la Veracruz (see page 76).

[fish in its broth]

Peel the apples and sprinkle them with the lemon juice. Wash the chiles, cut lengthwise and discard the seeds. Cut them in fine strips. Scald the tomatoes and peel them. Peel and chop the garlic and onions.

In a pan, bring 2 quarts of water to a boil. Add the tomatoes, onions, garlic, chiles, herbs and a pinch of salt. Cook for 30 minutes to make a court-bouillon. Rinse the fish and add it to the court-bouillon, when the onions are soft. Bring to a boil and cook for 5 minutes after it returns to boiling.

Remove the whiting with a slotted spoon, remove the skin, and return the fish to the broth. Add the apples cut in small sections. Cook for 5 minutes longer, without stirring, and serve immediately.

Serves 4
Prep time: 15 minutes
Marinating time: 4 hours
Refrigeration time:
at least 2 hours

3 firm apples
Juice of 1 lemon
8 small mild green chiles
4 large ripe tomatoes
3 cloves garlic
3 white onions
1 tablespoon dried oregano
1 tablespoon chopped
   fresh cilantro
2 tablespoons chopped
   fresh basil
1 sprig fresh thyme
2 bay leaves
Salt
1 whiting (2 pounds)
Salt

[ceviche]

Rinse the fish fillets and cut them in small pieces. Squeeze the limes. Put the fish in a porcelain dish and cover it completely with the lime juice. Marinate in the refrigerator for 4 hours. **S**cald the tomatoes, cool them, peel them and cut them in small chunks. Wash the chiles, cut them in half lengthwise and remove the seeds. Peel and mince the onion.

Remove the fish from the marinade, and drain them thoroughly on paper towels. Put them in a plate with the tomatoes, chiles, onion and chopped cilantro. Add salt and pepper and mix well. Refrigerate for at least 2 hours and, preferably, overnight.

When ready to serve the ceviche, add the olives and sprinkle with oregano.

Serves 4
Prep time: 15 minutes
Marinating time: 4 hours
Refrigeration time:
at least 2 hours

1 pound flounder fillets
   or white fish fillets
15 limes
3 tomatoes
4 small green chiles
1 onion
6 tablespoons chopped
   fresh cilantro
Salt and pepper
10 olives
2 teaspoons dried oregano

The following variation of a Spanish recipe can also be prepared with fillets of flounder or hake. The garlic must be golden brown but not burned—it is ready when it releases its aroma.

[fried fish with golden garlic]

Serves 4
Prep time: 10 minutes
Cooking time: 10 minutes
Marinating time: 1 hour

Salt and pepper
4 codfish fillets
  (5 ounces each)
Juice of 2 lemons
10 cloves garlic
3 tablespoons olive oil
3 tablespoons butter
Flour
½ bunch fresh parsley,
  chopped

Salt and pepper the fillets of fresh cod. Put them on a plate with the juice of 1½ lemons and allow them to marinate for 1 hour in the refrigerator.

Peel and slice the garlic cloves. Heat the olive oil and the butter in a nonstick pan and add the garlic. Sauté the garlic, over low heat, for 5 minutes, until it is golden brown. Remove the garlic but save the oil in the pan.

Dry the fillets of fish on paper towels, roll them in flour and fry them, 3 minutes on each side, in the garlic oil. Remove from the stove and add the remaining lemon juice, the sautéed garlic and chopped parsley. Cook for 2 minutes longer and serve without delay.

[trout with cilantro and red peppers]

Serves 4
Prep time: 20 minutes
Cooking time: 30 minutes

4 cleaned trout (5 ounces each)

For the stuffing:
¼ pound onion
6 ounces red bell peppers
⅓ cup butter
3–4 bread slices
1 bunch fresh cilantro
Salt
1 tablespoon tequila
2 lemons for juicing
⅓ cup bread crumbs
1 lemon for slices

Ask your fish vendor to remove the front and back fins. Rinse the fish.

Peel and mince the onions. Wash the bell peppers and remove the tops and the seeds. Cut the bell peppers in pieces. In a frying pan, sauté the onions in 1 tablespoon of the butter, over low heat, until they become transparent. Add the bell peppers and sauté them for 2–3 minutes.

Soak the bread slices in a bowl with cold water. Wash, dry and chop the cilantro. Add half of it to the frying pan as well as the salt, tequila, the juice of 2 lemons and then the drained bread. Mix all together and cook for 3–4 minutes over medium heat. Let it cool.

Preheat the oven to 500°F.

Stuff the trout, and then tie them with string to keep their shape. Put them in an ovenproof dish, and dot them with the remaining butter and sprinkle with the bread crumbs. Cook for 20–30 minutes in the oven.

Cut the last lemon in quarters and then in small wedges. Serve the trout sprinkled with fresh cilantro and the lemon wedges.

[seafood cocktail]

Cook the shellfish for 5 minutes in a pot of water, with a good amount of pepper added. Drain them and save ¼ cup of the cooking broth. Drain the broth and let it cool.

Shell the shrimp. In a salad bowl, mix the shrimp with the shellfish, the ¼ cup of reserved cooking broth, Mexican sauce, lemon juice, a few drops of Tabasco, the olive oil and ketchup. Toss well and refrigerate for 2 hours.

When ready to serve, add the sliced avocado and chopped cilantro.

Serves 4
Prep and cooking time:
30 minutes
Refrigeration time: 2 hours

1 pound shellfish
   (scallops, mussels, clams)
Pepper
16 large cooked shrimp
½ cup Mexican sauce
   (see page 26)
2 tablespoons lemon juice
A few drops Tabasco sauce
1 tablespoon olive oil
1 tablespoon ketchup
½ avocado
1 bunch fresh cilantro

Put the red beans in a pan with cold water and soak them overnight.

Next day, drain them and put them in a pan with 1½ quarts of water and bring it to a boil.

Peel the garlic and onion. Cut the onion in quarters and the bacon in small pieces. Add them all to the pan as well as the bouquet garni, salt and cloves. Cover and cook slowly, over low heat, for about 1 hour.

These beans are the perfect accompaniment to grilled chicken.

Serves 4
Prep time: 10 minutes
Cooking time: 1 hour
Soaking time: 12 hours

1 pound dried red beans
1 clove garlic
1 onion
3 ounces lean bacon
1 bouquet garni
(1 bay leaf, parsley stalks
  and 1 sprig fresh thyme;
  tied together with string)
Salt
2 cloves

[red beans mexican style]

Beans, and corn are main staples in Mexican cooking.

There are numerous varieties in all sizes and colors. In

this country, we can find the red ones, pintos (pink with

purple spots) and black ones. The latter must be placed

in cold water and boiled slowly, for about 2 hours. You

can add onion, oil, and jalapeño chile at the end to make

it complete.

[marinated shrimp and scallops]

Shell the shrimp carefully and put them in a porcelain dish. Open the scallops and clean them, dry them on paper towels and add them to the shrimp. Clean and save the empty shells (or use 12 shelled scallops).

Squeeze the lemons over a bowl to catch all the juice. Cover the seafood with the lemon juice, add the bouquet garni and marinate, in the refrigerator, for 4 hours, stirring from time to time.

Peel the onion and garlic and chop them finely. Wash the chiles, cut them in half lengthwise, discard the seeds and chop them finely. Rinse, dry and chop the cilantro. Mix together the chiles, garlic and onion, and a pinch of salt, pepper and chopped cilantro. Add the olive oil and stir. Add all these ingredients to the seafood marinade, mix well and put it in the refrigerator for 30 minutes.

Distribute the shrimp and the scallops, with their marinade, in the reserved shells or on small dishes, and serve well chilled.

Serves 4
Prep time: 30 minutes
Marinating time: 4 hours
Refrigeration time:
30 minutes

10 ounces shrimp
  in their shells
12 fresh scallops
4 lemons
1 bouquet garni
(1 bay leaf, parsley stalks
  and 1 sprig fresh thyme;
  tied together with string)
1 onion
1 clove garlic
3 hot small chiles
Salt and coarsely
  ground pepper
1 small bunch fresh cilantro
5 tablespoons olive oil

[fried zucchini with garlic]

Serves 4
Prep time: 40 minutes
Cooking time: 15 minutes

1 pound zucchini
Salt
6 cloves garlic
1 tablespoon oil
3 tablespoons
  butter, divided
Juice of 1 lemon
½ teaspoon crushed
  dried oregano
1 bunch fresh parsley

Wash the zucchini and cut them in ½ inch cubes. Mix them with 1 tablespoon of salt and let them drain in a colander for 30 minutes.

Rinse the zucchini with water and dry them in paper towels. Peel and mince the garlic.

Heat the oil and 1 tablespoon of the butter in a skillet. Stirring continuously, sauté the garlic over medium heat. Set aside. In the same pan, add the remaining butter and sauté the zucchini, over high heat, for 10 minutes—they should remain firm.

Remove from the heat, and mix the zucchini with the garlic, lemon juice, oregano and chopped parsley.

Serve warm as an accompaniment to grilled chicken.

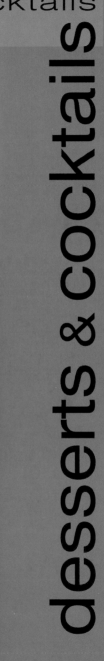

desserts & cocktails

desserts & cocktails

tropical sweets

If Mexican desserts were inspired by the Spaniards, then they have certainly adapted their native ingredients in their cooking. Limes, red bananas, mangoes, and let us not forget chocolate, which was not sweetened until the arrival of the Europeans. Simple to prepare, full of exotic aromas and caramelized sweets, these desserts will delight your guests.

[lime cream]

Serves 4
**Prep and cooking time:
1 hour
Refrigeration time: 3 hours**

6 gelatin sheets*
3 limes and their zests
¼ cup sugar
2 egg whites

Soak the gelatin sheets in cold water for 15 minutes (or see * below).

Brush 1 lime under cold water, dry it and finely grate the zest. Squeeze the juice from the other 2 limes.

Dissolve the sugar, over low heat, in ⅔ cup of water. Drain the gelatin and dissolve it in the sugared water. Add the lime juice and ¾ of the lime zest, reserving the remaining zest for use later as garnish. Stir and put in the refrigerator until the gelatin begins to set.

Whip the egg whites with a whisk until they form peaks. Beat the gelatin at half speed until it is creamy, and gently fold in the beaten egg whites. Refrigerate for 15 minutes.

Beat the cream again and put back in the refrigerator for 3 hours.

When firm, decorate with the rest of the lime zest and serve.

*Or dissolve 1 envelope gelatin in 3 tablespoons water for 5 minutes. Add, undrained, to dissolve in sugared water, as described above.

[rice fritters]

Serves 4
Prep and cooking time:
35 minutes

1 cup rice
¾ cup milk
½ cup sugar
2 eggs
½ cup bread crumbs
Oil for frying

Rinse the rice under running water. In a saucepan, bring the milk to a boil with half of the sugar and ⅓ cup of water. Add the rice and cook, over low heat, without stirring. Let it cool.

Beat the eggs lightly.

When the rice is completely cold, form small sausages (this is easier done with moist hands), rolling and shaping them in the palm of your hand. Dip them in the beaten egg, roll them in bread crumbs and fry for 5 minutes in hot oil. Drain them on paper towels before rolling them in the remaining brown sugar mixed with cinnamon.

Serve right away.

[coconut cake]

In a small saucepan, heat ⅓ cup of the sugar with 2 tablespoons water over medium heat, stirring continuously until the caramel becomes golden in color. Pour it into a mold, 10 inches in diameter, turning mold until the caramel covers the bottom and all the sides. When the caramel is hard, distribute the grated coconut in the mold.

Whip the eggs and the remaining sugar with an electric beater until the mixture is smooth and creamy. Add the evaporated milk and pour the mixture into the mold. Cover with aluminum foil.

Preheat the oven to 350°F.

Place the mold in a pan with water and bake it for 30 minutes. Remove the aluminum foil and bake for 30 minutes longer. Allow the cake to cool completely before covering it with plastic wrap. Refrigerate for 2 hours before serving. Serve it cold.

Serves 4
Prep time:
1 hour 15 minutes
Refrigeration time: 2 hours

1⅓ cups brown
   sugar, divided
⅓ cup grated coconut
3 eggs
1 cup evaporated milk

[mango dessert]

Serves 4
Prep time: 10 minutes
Refrigeration time: 1 hour

2 mangoes (1 pound each)
½ cup canned sweet
  condensed milk, or ½ cup
  milk cream (see page 112)
½ teaspoon freshly
  grated nutmeg
2 pinches ground cinnamon
A few drops vanilla extract
Coconut ice cream

Wash and peel the mangoes. Cut them in small pieces and mix them, in a glass bowl, with the condensed milk and nutmeg, cinnamon and a few drops of vanilla extract. Cover with plastic wrap and place in the refrigerator for, at least, 1 hour.

Serve with coconut ice cream sprinkled with a bit of cinnamon and nutmeg.

[fruit salad]

Serves 4
Prep time: 20 minutes
Refrigeration time:
30 minutes

1 lime
3 oranges
⅔ cup brown sugar
1 grapefruit
1 mango
1 small papaya
2 slices fresh pineapple

Brush the lime under running water and grate the zest.

Squeeze the juice of the lime and 1 of the oranges into a bowl. Dissolve the sugar in the citrus juice. Set aside.

Peel the 2 remaining oranges and the grapefruit. Cut them in sections.

Peel the mango and the papaya. Cut the pineapple, mango and papaya in chunks.

In a salad bowl, mix all the fruits and cover them with the reserved syrup. Refrigerate for 30 minutes and serve chilled.

[bananas flambé]

Squeeze the juice of the limes and the orange into a bowl. Wash and dry the bananas carefully and slice them without peeling them. Sprinkle banana slices with the citrus juice.
Melt the butter in a nonstick pan, and sauté the bananas for 2 minutes on one side. Turn them over, sprinkle them with sugar and cook them for 3 minutes. Pour the rum and, after 1 minute, ignite it and serve immediately.

Serves 4
Prep time: 5 minutes
Cooking time: 10 minutes

2 limes
1 orange
4 bananas
⅓ cup butter
2 tablespoons brown sugar
1 tablespoon dark rum

Serves 2
Prep time: 5 minutes

3 tablespoons grenadine
   syrup, plus a bit to coat
   rims of glasses
Powdered sugar
4 tablespoons white tequila
⅔ cup orange juice
8 ice cubes

[tequila sunrise]

Invert the rims of 2 tall glasses in a saucer with some grenadine syrup, and then invert them in a saucer with some powdered sugar to "ice" the rims with sugar.

Mix the tequila with the orange juice, divide it between the two glasses, and add ice cubes. Slowly pour 1½ tablespoons grenadine into each glass, without stirring—you will obtain the three colors of the sunrise.

[coffee liqueur]

Bring to a boil ⅔ cup of water with the cinnamon stick and ⅓ cup of the brown sugar. Let it boil for 5 minutes. Stir in the coffee and let it rest for 3 minutes.

Mix the rest of the sugar with the vanilla sugar in a glass bowl, add the egg yolks and whip with an electric beater until it becomes a light cream.

Set the bowl over a saucepan filled with simmering water (don't let the water touch the bottom of the bowl) to make a double boiler or "bain-marie," and cook, over low heat, for 30 minutes, beating the cream until it thickens. Add the milk, crème fraîche and rum followed by the coffee syrup. Cook for 5 minutes and let it cool.

Pour the coffee liqueur in a bottle and close the bottle tight.

You can keep this liqueur in the refrigerator for up to 6 months.

*Or use plain sugar and add ½ teaspoon vanilla when you add the milk.

Makes 2 cups liqueur
Prep time: 45 minutes

1 cinnamon stick
1 cup brown sugar, divided
2 tablespoons instant coffee
1 teaspoon vanilla
  flavored sugar*
6 egg yolks
⅓ cup milk
5 tablespoons crème fraîche
⅔ cup rum

[corn dessert]

Purée the corn in a food processor.

Bring to a boil the milk with the cinnamon stick and sugar, and cook until it becomes slightly thick. Add the corn purée and the raisins. Stir until it is thick, and pour the preparation in a deep dish.

Decorate it with grated coconut. Let it cool completely before covering it with plastic wrap and refrigerate for 1 hour.

Serves 4
Prep time: 10 minutes
Cooking time: 15 minutes
Refrigeration time: 1 hour

8 ounces canned corn
⅔ cup sweetened
  condensed milk
1 cinnamon stick
½ cup sugar
¼ cup raisins
¼ cup grated coconut

Dulce de leche, a sweet milk, is enjoyed in all parts of Latin America. In Mexico, it is traditionally prepared with goat milk and it is called cajeta. Sweetened evaporated milk, caramelized, is a convenient substitute.

[crêpes with
dulce de leche]

Serves 4
Prep and cooking time:
1 hour
Resting time: 1 hour

4 eggs
⅓ cup milk
1⅔ cup flour
¼ cup butter
½ cup dulce de leche
  (see page 112)

In a food processor, mix the eggs, milk and flour until it becomes a smooth batter. Let this crêpe batter rest for 1 hour at room temperature.
Stir the batter a couple of times just before using it. Melt the butter. In a lightly buttered, nonstick crêpe pan, pour a thin layer of batter and cook for 2 minutes on one side, and 2 minutes on the other. Make 12 crêpes in this manner.
Place 1 tablespoon of dulce de leche in the center of each crêpe, while still warm, and fold it in fourths toward the middle of the crêpe. Serve warm.

[pumpkin in syrup]

Serves 4
Prep time: 30 minutes
Cooking time:
1 hour 30 minutes

1 small pumpkin or other
winter squash
½ cup brown sugar or
maple syrup
1 vanilla pod
1 cinnamon stick

Cut the pumpkin in quarters, peel, and remove the seeds. Cut the flesh in big cubes.

In a large pan pour 1 quart of water, brown sugar, the vanilla pod split lengthwise and the cinnamon stick. Bring it to a boil and then cook slowly, for 20–30 minutes, until you obtain a thick syrup. Add the pumpkin cubes and toss to cover them well with the syrup.

Let them cool.

Preheat the oven to 300°F. Pour the pumpkin preparation in a baking dish and bake it for 1 hour and 30 minutes, turning the pumpkin in the syrup several times. Serve cold.

Peel the mangoes, remove the pit and cut the flesh in small cubes. Put mango cubes in a food processor with the lime juice, crème fraîche and powdered sugar. Process until it is a smooth cream. Distribute this cream in individual goblets, cover each one with plastic wrap and let it set in the refrigerator, for at least 2 hours.

Serves 4
Prep time: 15 minutes
Refrigeration time: 2 hours

2 very ripe large mangoes
Juice of 1 lime
⅔ cup crème fraîche
4 tablespoons powdered sugar

[mango mousse]

We should not be shocked to find sweet potatoes or

pumpkin, candied with sugar or syrup, eaten as desserts.

The cuisine of the Americas, the North as well as the

South, value these vegetables in sweet ways. There is not

enough space to complete the list: Tomatoes, peppers,

beans, chocolate and cassava are but a few of the

vegetables enjoyed as sweets.

[milk pudding]

In a pan, mix the baking soda with 1½ cups of the milk and cook only until it is a thick liquid, light brown in color. Add the remaining milk and the sugar, mix and cook for 2–3 hours, on very low heat, stirring as often as possible and scraping the bottom of the pan. Let it cool.

Serves 4
Prep time: 5 minutes
Cooking time:
at least 3 hours

½ teaspoon baking soda
1 quart whole milk
1 cup sugar

[sweet potatoes in syrup]

Wash the sweet potatoes and cook them for 30 minutes in boiling water. Preheat the oven to 300°F.

Cut the sweet potatoes in half, lengthwise. Make cuts in the flesh without piercing the skin. Insert pieces of butter in the openings. Put them in the oven and bake them until the sweet potatoes are a nice golden color.

Just before serving dot them with butter and drizzle the syrup on top. Serve warm.

Serves 4
Prep time: 15 minutes
Cooking time: 45 minutes

4 sweet potatoes
½ cup butter
½ cup light syrup

[egg liqueur]

Pour the milk in a pan, and add the cinnamon stick, peppercorns, clove, orange zest, sugar and baking soda. Bring to a boil over medium heat, then lower the heat and cook for 45 minutes, stirring all the time. Strain the milk through a mesh strainer and cool.

Beat the egg yolks and then, gradually, beat in the cooled milk. Thicken for 20 minutes, over low heat, without letting it boil. When the mixture is creamy, remove it from the heat and continue stirring until it is cold. Add the alcohol, pour it in a bottle and put it in the refrigerator for 1 hour. Serve very cold.

Makes 1 quart of liqueur
Prep time: 20 minutes
Cooking time:
about 1 hour
Refrigeration time: 1 hour

1 quart whole milk
1 cinnamon stick
4 peppercorns
1 clove
Zest of 1 orange
1¼ cups sugar
1 pinch baking soda
10 egg yolks
¼ cup rum or cognac

[pecan tart]

Melt the butter gently over low heat. In a bowl, mix the corn syrup with the sugar, melted butter, flour, 1 pinch of salt and the vanilla until you obtain a uniform mixture.

Beat the eggs lightly, add them to the mixture, followed by the pecans. Blend gently to combine.

Preheat the oven to 325°F. Line a buttered tart mold with the pie crust and add the pecan preparation. Put it in the oven and bake it for 50–55 minutes. To check if the tart is ready, insert the tip of a knife—it should come out clean.

Let cool before serving.

Serves 4
Prep time: 20 minutes
Cooking time:
50–55 minutes

¼ cup butter
⅓ cup corn syrup
1 cup sugar
2 tablespoons flour
Salt
1 teaspoon vanilla extract
3 eggs
6 ounces pecans
Butter to grease the
  tart mold
1 readymade pie crust
Salt

Serves 8–12
Special equipment:
9 x 13-inch cake pan
Prep time: 15 minutes
Cooking time:
30–40 minutes

1¾ cups flour
2 teaspoons baking powder
1 pinch baking soda
1 pinch salt
2 eggs
1⅔ cups brown sugar
⅓ cup oil, plus extra
  to oil baking pan
½ cup milk

[cake squares]

Preheat the oven to 350°F.

Mix together the flour, baking powder, baking soda and salt in a bowl. Beat the eggs lightly.

Combine brown sugar, eggs, oil and mix well. Add the dry ingredients and gently fold in, just until combined (don't overmix, or the cake will be heavy). Add the milk and gently fold in, again just until combined. Pour this batter into a lightly oiled 9 x 13-inch cake pan, and cook it in the preheated oven for 30–40 minutes, until cake springs back when lightly touched in the center.

Let the cake completely cool off before cutting it in small squares.

[glossary]

Banana leaves: fresh leaves used to make stuffed banana leaves: They can be replaced by baking paper or aluminum foil.

Beans: Mexican cooking uses mostly red beans, the most commonly used are pintos.

Cactus (nopales): impossible to find fresh outside of Mexico, but you can find them canned and cut into strips. The leaves that are used come from a thornless cactus, *Cactus opuntia*, which in Mexico is eaten cooked or raw.

Chayote: a kind of squash with a big pit. Its flesh resembles that of a potato. It is bought fresh and is eaten cooked or raw in salads.

Épazote: this herb is strong and bitter. It is used fresh or dried for cooking beans. It can be replaced with lemon grass.

Hot peppers: among the endless varieties of chiles, the most common are jalapeños and serranos, which are medium hot, and can be used powdered, fresh or canned.

Masa harina: a kind of flour made from dehydrated corn. It is the basis for corn tortillas.

Mole sauce: this sauce is made with about twenty ingredients, including chiles, dried fruits, chocolate and spices. It is one of the basics of Mexican cuisine. Its preparation is very complex and it is preferable to buy it in a jar.

Sweet potato: this large tuber can be yellow or pink and is native to South America. Its flesh is slightly sweet and can be cooked with salt or sugar.

Tomatillos: these little green tomatoes can be found canned or fresh. They cannot be replaced with unripe tomatoes.

Tortillas: these are made with corn or wheat flour. You can also make them (see page 11 and/or 28) for fresh, softer and better-tasting tortillas.

[shopping advice]

Typical Mexican Ingredients, such as tomatillos, masa harina, canned cactus, banana leaves or mole sauce, are not found exclusively in grocery stores that specialize in exotic products. They are now available in many local supermarkets. Sweet potatoes, tortillas, chayotes, chiles and red or black beans are readily available in produce stores, and in the produce section of most supermarkets. There are also grocers that specialize in the sale of Mexican products. In case you cannot find them, do not hesitate to inquire at your local Mexican restaurants.

glossary

[index]

Published originally under the title Bar Mexicain, ©2000 HACHETTE LIVRE (Hachette Pratique)

English translation for the U.S. market ©2001, Silverback Books, Inc.

Managing editors: Suyapa Audigier & Brigitte Éveno

Project editor: Lisa M. Tooker

Food editor: Terri Pischoff Wuerthner, CCP

Artwork and creation: Guylaine & Christophe Moi

Production: Nathalie Lautout & Patty Holden

Assistant editor: Sophie Brissaud

Editorial office: Sylvie Gauthier

Object photography: Matthieu Csech

Cover photo: Tony Stone Images/Bruce Herman

Photos: page 10 Sipa Press/Frilet, page 32 Diaf/Jean-Daniel Sudres, page 52 Hoaqui/Gerard Boutin, page 74 Tony Stone Images/Bruce Herman, page 96 Diaf/Jean-Daniel Sudres

ISBN : 1-930603-46-0

Printed and bound in Singapore.